Stage Struck

Stories linking with the History
National Curriculum Key Stage 2

First published in 1999 by Franklin Watts
96 Leonard Street, London EC2A 4XD

Editor: Sarah Snashall
Designer: Jason Anscomb
Consultant: Dr Anne Millard, BA Hons, Dip Ed, PhD

A CIP catalogue record for this book
is available from the British Library.

ISBN   0 7496 3363 8 (hbk)
       0 7496 3554 1 (pbk)

Dewey Classification 941.081

Printed in Great Britain

Stage Struck

by
Dennis Hamley
Illustrations by Martin Remphry

W

FRANKLIN WATTS
NEW YORK • LONDON • SYDNEY

1
Daisy's ambition

Daisy Welton, aged twelve, and her little
brother Alfie, two years younger, knew
they shouldn't be crouching by the side of
the stage at the Old Essex Music Hall in
London's East End so they could watch
the turns. Children shouldn't be anywhere

near such a rough place. Why, there weren't even many grown-up ladies here. Still, Father said they could watch – and Father was the Chairman.

Nearly all the people in the audience – sitting at their tables, drinking beer out of pewter tankards and smoking long, thin pipes so blue smoke filled the air with little billowing clouds – were men. But this was 1862. Men were in charge of everything and did exactly what they wanted. Women

kept quiet and knew their place.

They weren't much of an audience.
Half of them had their backs to the stage.
They were talking, shouting sometimes, as
waiters moved round the tables with trays
loaded with foaming tankards.

Look what they're missing, thought
Daisy. These men hardly knew that
Mr Harry Clifton was standing on the little
stage singing his own songs that Daisy
loved so much. Or that Mr George

Leybourne, dressed in singlet and shorts, was making those few who watched him laugh as he imitated the great Leotard, the wonderful trapeze artist. Mr Leybourne sang one of Daisy's favourite songs.

> *"He'd fly through the air with the*
> *greatest of ease,*
> *That daring young man on the*
> *flying trapeze.*
> *His movements were graceful,*
> *All girls he would please,*
> *And my love he purloin'd away."*

Oh, how Daisy felt for poor Mr Leybourne. And she felt even sorrier for her own father.

As Chairman of the music hall, Sam Welton sat at a table in front of the stage, banging his little hammer on the table in between turns and shouting, "Ladies and gentlemen, quiet please. Did you hear me? I said QUIET!" Then he banged the hammer louder than ever. "I have the great pleasure of announcing the next turn, brought here for your edification at ENORMOUS expense. Put your tankards down and pray silence. Give a big hand to your favourite and my favourite, THE GREAT VANCE." Then there would be a crashing chord from the piano, harmonium and drums. The handsome, curly-haired Mr Vance, resplendent in full evening dress of top hat and tails, would stride onto the stage, singing 'Pretty Polly, if you love me, do say yes.'

"It's nearly always men on the stage," Daisy sighed to Alfie.

★ ★ ★ ★

Then, one night, as he sat at the table eating a mutton chop, Sam Welton said, "You'll get a surprise tonight, Daisy."

"Oh, what is it?" cried Daisy.

"Wait and see," her father replied.

She didn't have to wait long. That evening, Daisy's father's voice boomed through the hall, "Put your hands together please for a little lady with a big heart, the sweet, the lovely MISS ANNIE ADAMS." Onto the stage came a dark-haired girl in a beautiful crinoline gown. Tuneful chords

sounded from the piano and Annie Adams'
lovely voice echoed through the hall singing,
"Are you gazing on this little beauty?"

Suddenly, there wasn't a whisper in
the hall. Not one man slopped his tankard,
not one man puffed smoke out of his pipe.
Nobody said a single word. Everyone
stared rapt at Miss Annie Adams.
When her song was over, they burst into
applause and roars of "Encore! Encore!"

Daisy, her eyes sparkling, turned to
Alfie and said, "That's what I want do
when I grow up."

2

A big chance?

The Old Essex Music Hall was built next to the pub in which Daisy, Alfie and her father lived, in rooms at the top. Daisy's mother had died when Alfie was born. Sam Welton had brought the two of them up himself.

Daisy loved standing alone in the hall by day. She loved the new chandeliers hanging from the high ceiling. She loved the galleries all round the walls which, at night, would be full of people. But most of all she loved the stage, its crimson curtains and the gas lamps which spread an exciting, mysterious glow across the performers.

Daisy stood on the stage, lost in wonderful dreams of her own. She imagined she too wore a lovely blue and silver crinoline dress and that, at the sight of her, there was silence in the hall. Then she imagined her father standing up, bringing his hammer down on the table and shouting, "Ladies and gentlemen, let's have the biggest welcome you've ever given to the best little lady of all, your favourite and my favourite, the lovely DAISY WELTON!"

The clapping and cheering would sound like waves on the seashore and when they died away she would be singing the very song Annie Adams sang –

'Are you gazing on this little beauty?'

But she wasn't imagining that part. She was really singing. Her clear, true voice travelled through the hall and she knew it reached every corner, right to the furthest point in the galleries. Oh, what a pity that she had to imagine the applause at the end.

She finished and curtseyed. The audience would have really loved it. But there was no audience.

Yes, there was. She heard footsteps at the back of the hall drawing nearer and a man's voice said, "Bravo!"

★ ★ ★ ★

The man walked towards the stage. He was smartly dressed in suit and waistcoat and he wore a top hat. As he approached her, he took the hat off, to show his shiny greying hair. Daisy could smell the sweetness of the pomade he used on it.

"Mursley's the name," he said as he held his hand out. "William Mursley. I manage the Harmonicum Hall in Whitechapel.

I know your father well. There's not a more respected man in the music halls than Sam Welton. I came to see him on a particular matter, but now I have something far more important to talk about."

Daisy looked at him, open-mouthed as she shook his hand.

"I tell you, that was the loveliest bit of singing I've heard for many a long day, and I've listened to the best, I can tell you. How would you like to appear at the Harmonicum Hall?"

"But I'm only twelve," she gasped.

"All the better," said Mr Mursley. "You'll be a bigger draw."

"You'll have to ask my father,"

Daisy replied. The very thought of the Harmonicum Hall frightened her. Ah, but if only she could …

* * * *

Sam Welton was very doubtful. "We'd never let anyone so young appear on stage at the Old Essex," he said. "Besides, I can't be there to look after her. We all know what some of the people who come to the halls are like."

"Don't worry, Sam," said Mr Mursley. "I'll see she's all right. You'll be very proud of her."

Sam Welton saw his daughter's sparkling eyes. His better judgment told him he was about to make a big mistake.

"I don't like it," Sam answered doubtfully.

"Don't worry," said Mr Mursley. "She'll be the toast of Whitechapel."

Sam looked again at his daughter's shining eyes and pleading expression. He gave in. "All right," he said. "She can go. But if anything bad happens I'll hold you responsible, William Mursley."

* * * *

3
Daisy's disaster

The Harmonicum Hall was smaller than
the Old Essex and was not as tidy and
shiny. There were no chandeliers, just
gaslamps round the walls. The curtains
were thin and patched and the piano was
out of tune. There was an unpleasant

smell of stale beer and unburnt coal gas. Excited though she was, Daisy knew that deep down she didn't like it.

Ten days had passed since Mr Mursley had made his offer. Daisy had practised and practised until she could sing her songs in her sleep. 'Are you gazing on this little beauty?' she *had* to sing. But Mr Mursley said Annie Adams' other songs were too grown-up. In the end, Daisy was to sing a sad, plaintive little ditty called 'Nobody's Child'.

Daisy nearly cried when she saw
what Mr Mursley had provided for her to
wear. No lovely crinoline ball
gown – she was to
appear as a little girl
with pinafore and
white stockings.
"You mustn't
look like Annie
Adams," said
Mr Mursley.
"You'd be too
knowing by half.
You'll look the
way I want you
to look."

The night of Daisy's performance
had arrived. She sat behind the stage
feeling sick. She wished she wasn't there.
She could hear the noise from the hall –

chattering, shouting and clinking of glasses which never stopped even when when the acts were on stage. Even backstage, tobacco smoke got into her throat.

It was her turn. She heard Mr Mursley rap the table with his hammer for quiet. Nobody seemed to take any notice. The noise carried on as bad as ever. She heard Mr Mursley shout, "And now, a special treat for one and all. Fresh from singing to all the crowned heads of Europe, the toast of every city in America," – the liar, thought Daisy – "I give you the sensation of the age, the child prodigy of the moment, the sweet, the fresh, the tuneful MISS DAISY WELTON!"

Then she found herself walking blindly on to the stage. In front was a confusion of blurred faces and blue smoke.

Still, she managed to start her song.

Her voice quavered and hardly seemed to cross the stage, but she managed the first line: "Are you gazing on this little beauty?"

"Not 'arf!" came a loud voice near the front and there was a burst of laughter. Then she saw a man stand up and point at Mr Mursley. "What's this, Bill?" he yelled. "Are you cradle-snatching?"

She couldn't continue. She saw
Mr Mursley and heard his voice above the
noise, "Go on to the second song."

She dimly heard the introduction on
the piano and then she started: "Nobody's
child, I'm nobody's child."

"I'm not surprised!" someone
shouted. Those round him laughed.
"Don't worry. You've got Bill Mursley to
look after you," called someone else. Now
the whole hall was rocking with laughter.

She stopped singing. Tears streamed down her face. Mr Mursley jumped on to the stage, seized her and bundled her off. She expected words of comfort, a kind voice telling her not to worry. Instead, he hissed, "You little fool. You've let me down."

★ ★ ★ ★

4

Getting over it

Sam Welton was very angry. "For two pins I'd kill that man," he roared. Then he calmed down and waves of remorse swept over him. "It's all my fault," he groaned. "I shouldn't have let her go."

As for Daisy, she had been put to

bed as soon as Mr Mursley's wife brought her home in a cab. For hours, she just couldn't sleep. Her head was swimming. All she heard were raucous, mocking voices from the audience. Tonight had

meant the end of all her dreams.

She would take more notice of the little school next to the church that the curate ran. She would learn her tables, study her reading books and try harder with her needlework. She would start work on an elaborate sampler. She'd use threads of many colours to stitch 'Lord bless this house'. She'd be like every other girl in Queen Victoria's reign.

★ ★ ★ ★

Sam had looked sadly at his daughter.

Poor Sam. He took no pleasure in his Chairman's duties. If it wasn't for the money, he would have given them up. But he might soon have to finish them anyway. The music hall was changing. The Old Essex was nice enough – but what was it really

but a big room stuck on the end of a pub? Why, in the West End of London, huge new music halls were being built, all gold paint and red plush. The audiences were smart. They didn't go just for a pot of ale and a smoke. They listened to the acts and the artists preferred playing to them. Soon there would be no place for the old-style Chairman.

Sam sighed. In many ways he wouldn't be sorry.

★ ★ ★ ★

A few weeks later, Daisy was sitting sewing when Alfie said to her, "I'm surprised at you, Daisy."

"Why?" she answered.

"Letting that horrible man put you down like that."

She looked at him with big, sad eyes.

"What can I do about it, Alfie?" she said.
"I'm only twelve."

"You've got to show him up."

Alfie was right. She shouldn't just
shrink away and forget all her dreams. And
she wouldn't. "One day," she said.

"'One day' isn't good enough, Daisy,"
said Alfie. "Do it now."

"If only I could," she said. Then anger swept through her. How dare that Mursley put her through so much. "I will, Alfie," she said. "I will."

"We'll do it together," Alfie replied. "What do you think of this?" He hummed a tune. "I don't know that one," she said.

"That's because I just wrote it."

Now it was her turn to stare at him. "Hum it again," she said.

Alfie's tune was lovely and catchy. "It needs some words."

"I know," Alfie replied. "Why don't you come to the piano with me and help me work some out."

"Yes," said Daisy. "Why not?"

Sam heard and saw all this and suddenly his heart was full of joy.

★ ★ ★ ★

After that night in the Harmonicum, Daisy thought she would never go in the Old Essex Hall again. But here she was, and Alfie was at the piano. He sat at the stool like a proper pianist. Wait till he starts his awful strumming, she thought.

But he didn't. He flexed his fingers,

then his hands closed over the keys and played the catchy tune he had hummed earlier.

"Who taught you to play like that?" she asked.

"Nobody. Taught myself, didn't I? Who taught you to sing?" He played a few more bars, then added, "It's in our blood."

Daisy listened carefully. Each separate note in the melody seemed to be trying to say a word to her.

"Play the tune again," she said.

"It's for a comic song," said Alfie. "We could be comedians together. A double act. Me at the piano, you singing and both of us telling jokes."

"What about?" said Daisy.

"William Mursley," Alfie answered.

★ ★ ★ ★

5

Rehearsing for revenge

It was wonderful. The moment Alfie said
the name – "William Mursley" – Daisy
said "Yes!" And for the rest of the day
Alfie was composing new tunes, Daisy was
finding words for them, jokes were written
down, sketches were improvised, and all

with one aim in mind – poking fun at William Mursley.

After three days they had put together and rehearsed a complete act. Alfie said, "Pa should see this."

So Daisy brought him in. He sat at a table at the front of the Hall. "So, what's this, then?" he asked.

Alfie came to the middle of the stage and said, "Ladies and gentlemen, we give you a new and amazing act, songs you'll never forget, jokes you'll never stop laughing at, from the sensational DAISY

AND ALFIE WELTON!" His high and piping voice sounded so different from the usual bellow announcing the acts that Sam found himself laughing already.

Alfie skipped back to the piano and played a loud chord. Then he started a catchy tune. Daisy entered from the wings and the lovely voice Sam knew well echoed through the empty hall.

> "I know a man, a silly, silly man
> Who tries too hard so you'll think
>   he's a card,
> And that's not all, 'cos he runs
>   another hall
> Which is all falling down, it's the
>   worst in the town."

Here, Daisy leaned forward as if she was sharing a secret with the audience.

"Ask no questions, hear no lies.
It would be a big surprise.
Shall I tell you? Yes I will.
Everyone – his name is – "

Here Alfie played another huge chord on the piano and Daisy formed her mouth into a big "O" and then sang "SWEET VI-OLETS".

Alfie stood at the piano and bowed, while Daisy curtsied. Sam stood up, clapping and shouting "Bravo!"

Now Alfie left the piano and came running up to Daisy. "I say, I say," he shouted. "What did the music hall Manager say when his hall was still empty just as his show was starting?"

"I don't know," said Daisy. "What did the music hall Manager say when the hall was still empty as his show was starting?"

"I wonder Har – moni will cum?" Alfie shouted.

"Did you hear what the music hall Chairman said when the girl singer had a bad cold?"

"No, I did not," Daisy replied.

"He asked the Manager, 'Is that her coughin'?' And the Manager answered, 'Yes, I keep one for all my acts to leave the stage in.'"

And so it went on, until Alfie said,
"Thank you, ladies and gentlemen. And

now, whether you know
who we've been talking
about or not, here's just
one final song to say
goodbye." He strode
back to the piano. A
few jaunty chords, then
Daisy came in.

"If the CAP FITS, WEAR IT.
That's all we've got to say
On this lovely, happy day.
If the CAP FITS, WEAR IT.
It's just one we're talking to,
Though I think that you'll know who.
If the CAP FITS, WEAR IT.
And that's all there is for now,
So we'll take our final bow,
If the CAP FITS, WEAR IT."

The last crashing chords came, Alfie stood and bowed, Daisy curtsied again and ran off the stage. Sam stood and cheered and the tears ran down his cheeks.

"That was grand," he called up to them. "And do you know what I'm going to do? I'm going to put you two on the bill next week, I'll tell Bill Mursley I've got a new mystery act he'd give his right arm to put on at the Harmonicum and I'll invite him round to see it. That might teach him a lesson."

Daisy felt very doubtful about this,

but Alfie said, "Go on, Daisy. We'll put him in his place."

So Daisy consented.

★ ★ ★ ★

The evening of the performance approached. All day Daisy felt very nervous, but she knew Bill Mursley needed to be shown up.

All the Essex regulars knew what had happened. When they saw William Mursley enter and sit at a table at the front with his tankard of ale and his pipe, there was muttering and a quiet hissing.

The acts went on: a singer, an

impersonator, a juggler.
Then it was their turn.

All was
prepared. Sam
turned to the
crowd. "And now,
at great expense, a
new act of rare talent,
the sensation of the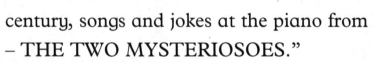
century, songs and jokes at the piano from
– THE TWO MYSTERIOSOES."

Alfie's rolling chord rang out, Daisy
tripped on to rousing applause and started
her song.

"I know a man, a silly, silly man ..."
She dared a look downwards and
saw William Mursley sitting there, his pipe
and tankard untouched and a look of
amazement on his face. The song ended
and there was a huge wave of applause

from an audience which, for a change, was listening attentively.

The act went on. The audience roared with laughter and William Mursley looked more and more uncomfortable. Now and again there was a shout: "That's caught you nicely, Bill Mursley." When the final song finished – 'If the CAP FITS, WEAR IT' – the applause and cheers filled the hall. Mursley stood up. His mouth opened, fish-like, as if he wanted to shout at the laughing crowd. But no sound came out, so he shook his

fist at everyone instead and stalked out.

Sam left his Chairman's table, and went over to Alfie and Daisy.

"That's finished him," Sam said. "He'll never live it down. Serves him right."

Then he looked at them seriously. "You two have real talent," he said. "In future I'll look after it properly. You've had one bad time. It won't be repeated. But you won't be doing your act here again."

"Why not? The Old Essex is lovely," said Daisy.

"I know," said Sam. "But the Old Essex is nearly finished. Along with all the places like it. The big new halls will carry the day." He paused and smiled. "Bill Mursley wasn't my only guest tonight."

A man Daisy had never seen before appeared and stood by Sam.

"Daisy and Alfie," said Sam. "May I introduce the most powerful music hall Manager in London. Mr Charles Morton."

"I'm very pleased to meet you," said Mr Morton gravely. "I was very impressed. You'll go a long way, the two of you. You'll hear from me again."

★ ★ ★ ★

6

On a bigger stage

Now began an exciting time. When will we hear from Mr Morton? The question kept running through Daisy's mind.

"Don't worry, you will," said Sam. "Charles Morton is a man of his word."

Meanwhile, they spent every day rehearsing and composing. Alfie wrote the tunes and Daisy fitted words to them all.

Then one day, two months after Daisy's thirteenth birthday, Mr Morton came again. "No, it's not to tell you when I've booked you," he said. "I just want to hear how you're getting on."

They played their new songs to him. He listened, smiling and tapping his foot. Yes, he liked them. "But, Daisy," he said. "I've heard a lot about you. Annie Adams is your favourite singer, isn't she?"

"Well, yes," said Daisy.

"She's one of mine, too. Didn't you once sing a song of hers?"

"Yes," said Daisy reluctantly. " 'Are you gazing on this little beauty?' But I don't like to ..."

"I know. It reminds you of that awful

night. Don't worry, I know all about it.
But, Daisy, would you sing it for me now?
Can you remember it?"

How could she ever forget it?

"I can play it," said Alfie.

So, tremblingly at first, then with
more confidence, she sang – that song

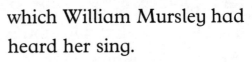

which William Mursley had heard her sing.

There was silence when she finished. She looked at Mr Morton. He doesn't like it, she thought.

But he did. "Daisy," he said, "I want you to sing a song like that just for me. Not someone else's, but yours and yours alone. Not a comic song but a real ballad that can show your beautiful voice off properly."

"I'll write one," cried Alfie excitedly.

★ ★ ★ ★

Three days later, that's just what he'd done. A lovely melody which Daisy found so easy to put words to. These words, she knew, were really all about what she felt after running off the stage at the Harmonicum Hall but how, with Alfie's help, she fought back and not let William Mursley get her down.

A month later, Mr Morton came back to the Old Essex.

★ ★ ★ ★

One night, Daisy watched a lovely set of performances. Daisy had listened and ached to be on the stage with them, especially now the audiences seemed to be getting better at paying attention.

But when the show was over, Sam said, "Look who's here."

Yes, Mr Morton was back again.

"Daisy, he said. "I had engaged a singer for my Oxford Music Hall whom you admire very much. Can you guess who?"

There could only be one answer. "Annie Adams," she said faintly.

"But guess what's happened. She's lost her voice, so I need a deputy turn. Who could I ask to help me?"

"Kate Harley?" suggested Daisy.

"Jenny Smith?' suggested Alfie.

"I could," said

Mr Morton, "but I was hoping for someone new, a fresh sensation for the country's stages. Who could that be, I wonder?"

Daisy's mouth felt dry. She could not say a word.

Mr Morton laughed. "I salute you both. Welcome to the Oxford Music Hall and careers in which your names will ring across the world."

★ ★ ★ ★

Daisy had never seen anything like the Oxford Music Hall. It was huge. The stalls sloped upwards from the stage and the orchestra pit, while the balconies sloped downwards, so it seemed anyone sitting in them must fall over the edge. Why, over a thousand people could crowd in, and every eye would be focused on the figures on the stage. All was gilt and red plush, with ornate mouldings, rich heavy curtains and chandeliers which gleamed and twinkled. It was a truly magic place.

★ ★ ★ ★

That evening, the Chairman of the Oxford Music Hall announced: "My lords, ladies

and gentlemen, I crave your indulgence for a new act, guaranteed to become your favourite for many years ahead. For songs at the piano with a wit and freshness such as you have not heard for many a long year, I give you – DAISY AND ALFIE WELTON."

The curtains opened and there they were, an audience quiet and intent. Alfie's music sounded clear and pure and Daisy began the song they had written together

which was to make their names for ever.

"Once I was just a little girl lost,
On waves of grief I was tumbled
and toss'd,
But now I know that the world
wears a smile,
And while I cried it was there all
the while."

The first verse with Alfie's unforgettable, flowing melody was over. Now began the chorus, calm and confident.

"So sing with me,
So fly with me,
But whatever happens,
Don't cry with me ..."

When they had finished, waves of applause crossed the orchestra pit to the two small figures on the stage. Daisy's dream had come true at last.

Music Halls

Beginnings

People have always liked a good song and a story.
The first music halls were small places in or
attached to taverns and 'polite' people kept away
from them. Even so, singers from respectable places
such as Covent Garden
Theatre often earned
some extra money
singing in these new
music halls. By 1850
the halls and the big
theatres existed side by
side.

The halls

There were big
differences between
early music halls and theatres. One was that in the
theatre you went to watch and listen, while in the
halls you could go on drinking and talking and the
waiters would carry on serving, even while the acts

were performing. Another was that the halls were not licensed for dramatic performances. Though comedians could tell their jokes, nothing like actual plays could be put on. The music halls got away with little sketches – but anything more and the proprietors were up in court and fined.

The Chairman

The Chairman was very important. He introduced the turns and kept order. This was often difficult. The Chairman only disappeared when the new halls became very large, and audiences came to listen rather than drink, and programmes were sold.

The turns

Many names of turns from the great days of the music hall are still remembered – Dan Leno, George Robey, 'Little Tich', Marie Lloyd, and many, many more. Their songs are still sung, for

MARIE LLOYD

example: 'My old man said follow the van and don't dilly-dally on the way', and 'Boiled beef and carrots'.

The things the Victorian audiences found funny might leave us cold today. They loved puns, and any plays on words. The two jokes Alfie and Daisy tell about Bill Mursley are typical. Say 'Har – moni will cum?' out loud. It sounds like, 'How many will come?' Believe it or not, they'd have died laughing at that. And in the next joke – 'coughin'' sounds like 'coffin'.

Bigger and better

As the 19th century went on, more and more music halls were built. To cram more people in, they became bigger, plusher, more comfortable and much more like proper theatres. Powerful managers became famous for the shows they put on. Charles Morton was a real person and he was the first of these powerful people. Every city had several music halls. Some are still there, refurbished and used by big theatre and opera companies. In London there were scores. Many were destroyed in the Second World War, but some, like the Victoria Palace, the Palladium, the Palace Theatre, still stand. Theatres like the Old Vic and Sadlers Wells started life as music halls.

Nowadays

Though film, radio and then television killed off the old music hall, the traditions still live on. In clubs up and down the country, in the seaside shows and on television and radio, comedians and singers still entertain us, much as those old music hall performers did years ago.

Sparks: Historical Adventures

ANCIENT GREECE
The Great Horse of Troy – The Trojan War
0 7496 3369 7 (hbk)   0 7496 3538 X (pbk)
The Winner's Wreath – Ancient Greek Olympics
0 7496 3368 9 (hbk)   0 7496 3555 X (pbk)

INVADERS AND SETTLERS
Boudicca Strikes Back – The Romans in Britain
0 7496 3366 2 (hbk)   0 7496 3546 0 (pbk)
Viking Raiders – A Norse Attack
0 7496 3089 2 (hbk)   0 7496 3457 X (pbk)
Erik's New Home – A Viking Town
0 7496 3367 0 (hbk)   0 7496 3552 5 (pbk)
TALES OF THE ROWDY ROMANS
The Great Necklace Hunt
0 7496 2221 0 (hbk)   0 7496 2628 3 (pbk)
The Lost Legionary
0 7496 2222 9 (hbk)   0 7496 2629 1 (pbk)
The Guard Dog Geese
0 7496 2331 4 (hbk)   0 7496 2630 5 (pbk)
A Runaway Donkey
0 7496 2332 2 (hbk)   0 7496 2631 3 (pbk)

TUDORS AND STUARTS
Captain Drake's Orders – The Armada
0 7496 2556 2 (hbk)   0 7496 3121 X (pbk)
London's Burning – The Great Fire of London
0 7496 2557 0 (hbk)   0 7496 3122 8 (pbk)
Mystery at the Globe – Shakespeare's Theatre
0 7496 3096 5 (hbk)   0 7496 3449 9 (pbk)
Plague! – A Tudor Epidemic
0 7496 3365 4 (hbk)   0 7496 3556 8 (pbk)
Stranger in the Glen – Rob Roy
0 7496 2586 4 (hbk)   0 7496 3123 6 (pbk)
A Dream of Danger – The Massacre of Glencoe
0 7496 2587 2 (hbk)   0 7496 3124 4 (pbk)
A Queen's Promise – Mary Queen of Scots
0 7496 2589 9 (hbk)   0 7496 3125 2 (pbk)
Over the Sea to Skye – Bonnie Prince Charlie
0 7496 2588 0 (hbk)   0 7496 3126 0 (pbk)
TALES OF A TUDOR TEARAWAY
A Pig Called Henry
0 7496 2204 4 (hbk)   0 7496 2625 9 (pbk)
A Horse Called Deathblow
0 7496 2205 9 (hbk)   0 7496 2624 0 (pbk)
Dancing for Captain Drake
0 7496 2234 2 (hbk)   0 7496 2626 7 (pbk)
Birthdays are a Serious Business
0 7496 2235 0 (hbk)   0 7496 2627 5 (pbk)

VICTORIAN ERA
The Runaway Slave – The British Slave Trade
0 7496 3093 0 (hbk)   0 7496 3456 1 (pbk)
The Sewer Sleuth – Victorian Cholera
0 7496 2590 2 (hbk)   0 7496 3128 7 (pbk)
Convict! – Criminals Sent to Australia
0 7496 2591 0 (hbk)   0 7496 3129 5 (pbk)
An Indian Adventure – Victorian India
0 7496 3090 6 (hbk)   0 7496 3451 0 (pbk)
Farewell to Ireland – Emigration to America
0 7496 3094 9 (hbk)   0 7496 3448 0 (pbk)

The Great Hunger – Famine in Ireland
0 7496 3095 7 (hbk)   0 7496 3447 2 (pbk)
Fire Down the Pit – A Welsh Mining Disaster
0 7496 3091 4 (hbk)   0 7496 3450 2 (pbk)
Tunnel Rescue – The Great Western Railway
0 7496 3353 0 (hbk)   0 7496 3537 1 (pbk)
Kidnap on the Canal – Victorian Waterways
0 7496 3352 2 (hbk)   0 7496 3540 1 (pbk)
Dr. Barnardo's Boys – Victorian Charity
0 7496 3358 1 (hbk)   0 7496 3541 X (pbk)
The Iron Ship – Brunel's Great Britain
0 7496 3355 7 (hbk)   0 7496 3543 6 (pbk)
Bodies for Sale – Victorian Tomb-Robbers
0 7496 3364 6 (hbk)   0 7496 3539 8 (pbk)
Penny Post Boy – The Victorian Postal Service
0 7496 3362 X (hbk)   0 7496 3544 4 (pbk)
The Canal Diggers – The Manchester Ship Canal
0 7496 3356 5 (hbk)   0 7496 3545 2 (pbk)
The Tay Bridge Tragedy – A Victorian Disaster
0 7496 3354 9 (hbk)   0 7496 3547 9 (pbk)
Stop, Thief! – The Victorian Police
0 7496 3359 X (hbk)   0 7496 3548 7 (pbk)
A School – for Girls! – Victorian Schools
0 7496 3360 3 (hbk)   0 7496 3549 5 (pbk)
Chimney Charlie – Victorian Chimney Sweeps
0 7496 3351 4 (hbk)   0 7496 3551 7 (pbk)
Down the Drain – Victorian Sewers
0 7496 3357 3 (hbk)   0 7496 3550 9 (pbk)
The Ideal Home – A Victorian New Town
0 7496 3361 1 (hbk)   0 7496 3553 3 (pbk)
Stage Struck – Victorian Music Hall
0 7496 3363 8 (hbk)   0 7496 3554 1 (pbk)
TRAVELS OF A YOUNG VICTORIAN
The Golden Key
0 7496 2360 8 (hbk)   0 7496 2632 1 (pbk)
Poppy's Big Push
0 7496 2361 6 (hbk)   0 7496 2633 X (pbk)
Poppy's Secret
0 7496 2374 8 (hbk)   0 7496 2634 8 (pbk)
The Lost Treasure
0 7496 2375 6 (hbk)   0 7496 2635 6 (pbk)

20th-CENTURY HISTORY
Fight for the Vote – The Suffragettes
0 7496 3092 2 (hbk)   0 7496 3452 9 (pbk)
The Road to London – The Jarrow March
0 7496 2609 7 (hbk)   0 7496 3132 5 (pbk)
The Sandbag Secret – The Blitz
0 7496 2608 9 (hbk)   0 7496 3133 3 (pbk)
Sid's War – Evacuation
0 7496 3209 7 (hbk)   0 7496 3445 6 (pbk)
D-Day! – Wartime Adventure
0 7496 3208 9 (hbk)   0 7496 3446 4 (pbk)
The Prisoner – A Prisoner of War
0 7496 3212 7 (hbk)   0 7496 3455 3 (pbk)
Escape from Germany – Wartime Refugees
0 7496 3211 9 (hbk)   0 7496 3454 5 (pbk)
Flying Bombs – Wartime Bomb Disposal
0 7496 3210 0 (hbk)   0 7496 3453 7 (pbk)
12,000 Miles From Home – Sent to Australia
0 7496 3370 0 (hbk)   0 7496 3542 8 (pbk)